W9-CAN-889

CUB REPORTER MEETS FAMOUS AMERICANS

WHAT'S YOUR STORY, CESAR CHAVEZ?

Emma Carlson Berne
illustrations by Doug Jones

Lerner Publications ◆ Minneapolis

Note to readers, parents, and educators:
This book includes an interview of a famous American. While the words this person speaks are not his actual words, all the information in the book is true and has been carefully researched.

Text and illustrations copyright © 2016 by Lerner Publishing Group, Inc.

All rights reserved. International copyright secured. No part of this book may be reproduced, stored in a retrieval system, or transmitted in any form or by any means—electronic, mechanical, photocopying, recording, or otherwise—without the prior written permission of Lerner Publishing Group, Inc., except for the inclusion of brief quotations in an acknowledged review.

Lerner Publications Company
A division of Lerner Publishing Group, Inc.
241 First Avenue North
Minneapolis, MN 55401 USA

For reading levels and more information, look up this title at www.lernerbooks.com.

Main body text set in Avenir LT Pro 45 Book 15/21. Typeface provided by Linotype AG.

Library of Congress Cataloging-in-Publication Data

Berne, Emma Carlson.
    What's your story, Cesar Chavez? / by Emma Carlson Berne.
        pages cm. — (Cub reporter meets famous Americans)
    Audience: Ages 5–9.
    ISBN 978-1-4677-7967-8 (lb : alk. paper) — ISBN 978-1-4677-8537-2 (pb : alk. paper) — ISBN 978-1-4677-8538-9 (eb pdf)
    1. Chavez, Cesar, 1927-1993—Juvenile literature. 2. Labor leaders—United States—Biography—Juvenile literature. 3. Mexican American migrant agricultural laborers—Biography—Juvenile literature. 4. Agricultural laborers—Labor unions—United States—History—Juvenile literature. 5. United Farm Workers—History—Juvenile literature.
    I. Title.
HD6509.C48B47 2016
331.88'13092—dc23 [B]   2015000424

Manufactured in the United States of America
1 – VP – 7/15/15

Table of Contents

Hi, everyone! Today, I'm interviewing a very important person. His name is Cesar Chavez. Cesar, can you tell us a little about yourself?

Cesar says: Of course. I was a **labor** leader starting in the 1950s. I helped farm workers join together so that they could get better pay and better working **conditions**. At that time, workers on farms made very little money. They had to work for many hours in the hot sun, and farm owners treated them badly. I organized a **union** made up of farm workers. The union helped the workers stand up for their rights.

Cesar Chavez spent forty years fighting for workers' rights.

Where and when were you born?

Cesar says: I was born in 1927 in Arizona. My parents were farmers. Their parents had come from Mexico. My mother always told my brothers and sisters and me how important it was to help other people. She told us we should walk away from fights, and she made all of us share our food equally.

When I was ten, we had to leave our farm. We could not afford to keep it. After that, we were poor. We traveled around, picking crops for other farmers. Later, we lived in a garage in a poor part of San Jose, California.

Cesar grew up on a farm like this one in Yuma, Arizona. In the 1930s, bad harvests made life difficult for farmers. Many farmers lost their land.

What was it like to be a farm worker?

Cesar says: It was very hard. I had loved living and working on my family's farm. But the big farms where we worked were different. Workers had to do whatever the farm owners told them. And many owners made people work in terrible conditions. Workers might have to pay for their drinking water. And there was no place to use the toilet.

When Cesar was a child, the children of farm workers—such as these kids—often had to work with their parents.

Why didn't anyone complain about the conditions farm workers faced?

Cesar says: Most people were afraid to complain. Many farm workers were Mexican Americans, like my family, or recent **immigrants** from Mexico. White people often treated Mexican Americans unfairly. It was hard for us to get work. When we did have jobs, we didn't want to lose them. And if we complained, we could be fired. So workers stayed quiet and tried not to make their bosses angry.

This family of farm workers made a temporary home near Harlingen, Texas, in 1939. Families often moved from farm to farm, looking for work. They had no permanent homes.

When did you start trying to help farm workers?

Cesar says: In 1952, I met a man named Fred Ross. Fred was the leader of a group called the Community Service Organization (CSO). The CSO helped Mexican American people fight for their rights and stand up for themselves. I started working for Fred. Soon I was the director of the CSO. But I wanted to do more.

The CSO tried to help Mexican American workers in many ways. But different kinds of workers had different needs. So I decided to make a union for just one group: farm workers.

Cesar spoke to many people who wanted to stand up for their rights.

Why did you want to organize farm workers?

Cesar says: Since I had been a farm worker, I knew what a hard life it could be. Workers wanted enough money to buy food and clothes. They wanted safe, comfortable places to live and work. But they could not make their bosses listen to them.

I knew people were stronger when they worked together. So my friend Dolores Huerta and I created a union called the National Farm Workers Association (NFWA). Farm workers who joined my union agreed that they would ask for the same things, all at once. If their bosses didn't agree, the workers would have a **strike**. Then the bosses would *have* to make changes, or they'd be left with no workers.

Labor leader Dolores Huerta *(left)* teamed up with Cesar *(right)* to create a farm workers' union.

When was your first strike?

Cesar says: Our union had its first big strike in 1965. Grape growers in California decided to pay workers even less money than usual during the grape harvest—the busiest time for work. Our union joined with another union. Together, all the workers walked out of the fields. We refused to pick grapes until the growers agreed to pay us a fair amount. About a year into the strike, the NFWA and the other union became the United Farm Workers (UFW). For four years, I led the workers as they refused to pick grapes.

In 1966, Cesar *(center)* organized a protest march from Farmersville, California, to Sacramento, California, the state's capital. The journey was 300 miles (483 kilometers) long.

Who supported the strike?

Cesar says: Lots of people did! We also asked people all around the country to **boycott** grapes. We explained that workers were being treated badly. We asked Americans not to support grape growers until the growers treated their workers better. Thirteen million Americans stopped buying grapes during the boycott.

Cesar, holding a Don't Buy California Grapes! sign, stands outside of a supermarket in 1966.

Who was unhappy about the strike?

Cesar says: Some people thought that we should not try to damage the grape growers' business. Politicians—including the governor of California and the president of the United States—believed we were hurting American farming in general. Governor Ronald Reagan even ate grapes in public to show that he did not agree with the boycott.

Some politicians disliked Cesar's work. But others supported him. In this 1968 photo, New York senator Robert F. Kennedy *(front left)* sits next to Cesar at a UFW rally.

Did the strike work?

Cesar says: It did! In 1970, the grape growers agreed to sign new **contracts** with union workers. The contracts said workers would be paid more money.

After the grape strike, I led other strikes. I also organized **pickets**. At these protests, people could gather near where they usually worked. They tried to convince other workers to join the strike. Pickets were covered in the news across the country. People all around the United States heard or read about the protests—and the reasons behind them. This helped us get support. But it was still hard to achieve our goals.

The UFW reached an agreement with grape growers in 1970. Cesar *(front left)* and grape grower John Giumarra Sr. *(front center)* signed a contract. Then they exchanged pens to show they had a partnership.

What new problems did you face?

Cesar says: Grape growers had promised to pay UFW members fairly. But they had not promised to actually hire UFW members in the first place. Instead, they hired members of another union, the Teamsters. Lettuce growers did the same thing. The Teamsters worked for much lower pay. And UFW members lost their jobs.

We organized more strikes and protests to get fair pay. But a lot of union members were arrested for picketing. The government was not protecting our right to have a union and stand up for ourselves.

Eventually, the Teamsters and the UFW came to an agreement. But I could see that our rights were still in danger.

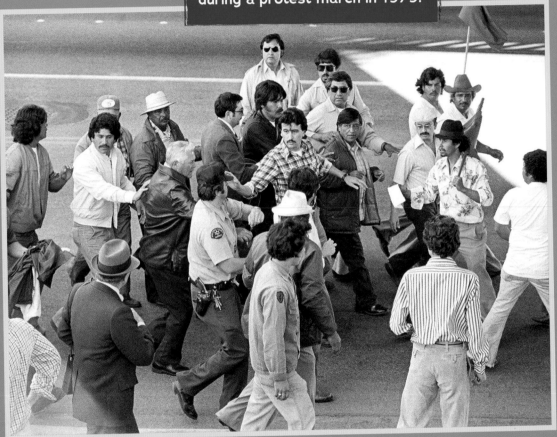

A sheriff's deputy *(front center)* approaches Cesar *(center right)* during a protest march in 1979.

What did you do next?

Cesar says: I wanted our union to be protected by law. Then union members would not be arrested for joining a strike or a protest. So I talked to California's leaders. I helped convince them to pass a law that would protect every farm worker's right to be in a union. This law was called the Agricultural Labor Relations Act. In June 1975, the act took effect. Farm workers now had the legal right to join together, make deals with their employers for better pay, and demand better working conditions.

But my work wasn't done. I never stopped trying to help workers have better lives. And the UFW still exists. It has set an example for other kinds of workers. Those workers have organized their own unions.

Cesar *(front)* marches with UFW members outside a supermarket. The UFW often picketed businesses that sold products harvested by underpaid workers.

How are modern workers' lives better because of you?

Cesar says: These days, many workers on farms, in factories, and in stores earn more money and work in safer, more comfortable conditions. And if they don't get these things, they can speak up through their union. I told the world that workers deserve the right to speak up—and that this right should be protected by law.

But other workers still labor in poor conditions. They are paid very little. They might be afraid that their bosses will punish them or fire them if they say anything. The work I started isn't finished. People continue to fight for fairer treatment.

Timeline

1927: Cesar Chavez is born in Arizona.

1938: The Chavez family loses their farm and must become farm workers.

1948: Cesar marries Helen Fabela. Eventually, they had eight children.

1952: Cesar meets Fred Ross and joins the Community Service Organization.

1962: Cesar forms the National Farm Workers Association, a labor union.

1965: The NFWA joins with another union and begins the strike against grape growers.

1970: California grape growers agree to sign contracts that protect workers' rights and pay. The union, now called the UFW, ends the strike.

1970–1973: The UFW organizes other strikes and protests.

1975: The Agricultural Labor Relations Act is passed in California.

1993: Cesar Chavez dies. Fifty thousand people attend his funeral.

Glossary

boycott: to stop buying goods or doing a certain activity as a form of protest

conditions: the situation in which someone lives or works. Conditions might include the environment, the weather, and the types of tasks someone has to do.

contracts: written agreements that promise certain things

immigrants: people who move from one country to live in another country

labor: work that often involves physical activity and is performed by workers to earn money

pickets: events where union workers and other protesters gather and try to convince other workers to join a strike

strike: when a group of workers all refuse to work in the hope of gaining certain rights or conditions

union: an organization of workers that stands up for the rights of its members

LERNER

e

SOURCE™

Expand learning beyond the printed book. Download free, complementary educational resources for this book from our website, www.lerneresource.com.

Further Information

Books

Adler, David A., and Michael S. Adler. *A Picture Book of Cesar Chavez.* New York: Holiday House, 2010. Pictures help tell this story of Cesar Chavez's life.

Barton, Jen. *What's Your Story, Harriet Tubman?* Minneapolis: Lerner Publications, 2016. Join the Cub Reporter to learn about another leader who fought for fair treatment and equal rights.

Brown, Monica. *Side by Side/Lado a Lado: The Story of Dolores Huerta and Cesar Chavez.* New York: Rayo, 2010. Using both English and Spanish, this story tells how Cesar Chavez and Dolores Huerta teamed up to help workers.

Macceca, Stephanie E. *Cesar Chavez: Protecting Farm Workers.* Huntington Beach, CA: Teacher Created Materials, 2011. Learn more about how Cesar Chavez helped farm workers gain their rights.

Websites

The Biography of Cesar Chavez
http://chavez.cde.ca.gov/ModelCurriculum/Teachers/Lessons/Resources/Biographies/K-2_Bio.aspx
This site from California's government has lots of pictures of Cesar Chavez and describes his life.

Meet Amazing Americans: Cesar Chavez
http://www.americaslibrary.gov/aa/chavez/aa_chavez_subj.html
Learn more about Cesar Chavez on this Library of Congress site.

Index

Photo Acknowledgments

The images in this book are used with the permission of: © Arthur Schatz/The LIFE Picture Collection/Getty Images, pp. 5, 15; © Folio/Alamy, p. 7; Library of Congress, pp. 9, 11; Library of Congress, p. 11; © Ted Streshinsky/CORBIS, p. 13; AP Photo, p. 17; AP Photo/Barry Sweet, p. 19; © Michael Rougier/The LIFE Picture Collection/Getty Images, p. 21; © Bettmann/CORBIS, p. 23; AP Photo/Paul Sakuma, p. 25; AP Photo/Walter Zeboski, p. 27.

Cover: © Najlah Feanny/CORBIS.